THE ART OF STEPPING THROUGH TIME

THE ART OF STEPPING THROUGH TIME

Selected Poems

H.E. Sayeh

Translated from Persian
by Chad Sweeney and Mojdeh Marashi

WHITE PINE PRESS / BUFFALO, NEW YORK

Publication of this book was made possible, in part, with public funds from the New York State Council on the Arts, a State Agency, and by grants from the National Endowment for the Arts, which believes that a great nation deserves great art, and the Witter Bynner Foundation.

ACKNOWLEDGMENTS:
American Letters & Commentary: "Night's Alley"
Atlanta Review: "Caravan"
Crazyhorse: "Life," "Fear (Holl)," and "A Few Thousand Hopes of the Children of Adam"
Fourteen Hills: "Red and White" and "Number"
Indiana Review: "The Art of Stepping Through Time" and "Black and White"
Ping Pong: Henry Miller Library Journal: "Kayvaan was a Star," "Apple's Cry," "Red Dawn," "Design," "The Fall," "Death of the Day," "The Bird Knows" and "Cry"
Poetry International: "Exiled" (as "Search/Circle") and "Moan of the Mirror"
Seattle Review: "Story," "Maybe," and "Dove's Wings"
Subtropics: "Sunset on the Green"
Washington Square Journal: "Arghavaan"
    The poems "Caravan" and "The Art of Stepping Through Time" were printed in the anthology *Forbidden Poems, Iran and Its Exiles* (Michigan State University Press, 2011), edited by Sholeh Wolpe.
    The poem "The Art of Stepping Through Time" was published as a limited edition, letter-pressed art book with artist Ala Ebtekar at the San Francisco Center for the Book.
    The San Francisco Arts Commission awarded the project a Cultural Equities Grant in 2008 for which we are deeply grateful. We would like to express our gratitude to all the fine organizations whose support was crucial to this project and to so many others.

First Edition.

ISBN: 978-1-935210-27-6

Printed and bound in the United States of America.

Library of Congress Control Number: 2011931992

White Pine Press
P.O. Box 236, Buffalo, New York 14201
www.whitepine.org

CONTENTS

II. 1971-1980

III. 1946-1970

PREFACE

Mojdeh Marashi and I began this *Selected Poems of H.E. Sayeh* (Houshang Ebtehaj) in 2003 with the remarkable poem "Arghavaan." Mojdeh provided a rough translation from the Persian as well as thorough etymological, cultural, and historic notes—and my job was to complete the poem in English. I was working alone, past midnight, when Mojdeh's syllable-by-syllable notes began to puzzle their way into meaning. I was awed by the difficulties of translating contemporary Persian into English, for the syntactical reversals and tightly wound cultural references. The voice in "Arghavaan" was speaking from a prison cell, where a "thin flame from a sick lamp/ is the only storyteller tonight." Sayeh had been arrested two years after the Islamic Revolution of 1979, and from the darkness of the state dungeon, he had a vision of the tree in his front yard, the Arghavaan, the first tree to bloom in the spring. The tree arose from memory and imagination as a link to his family: "Arghavaan! . . . Become my bleeding poem . . . Shout the poem I cannot write." I was moved, both for the poem's passionate cry and for its Persian *deep image*, as old as the world itself and what seemed to be a kindred spirit to Lorca's Andalusian *duende*. At that moment I commited to deliver an entire book of Sayeh's poetry into English, as if this act alone could retroactively open the door to Sayeh's cell and return him to the world. For the next eight years Modjeh and I worked closely on selecting and translating the poems for this collection. Mojdeh spoke on the phone with Sayeh for countless hours and flew to both Germany and Iran to work with the poet directly.

9

H.E. Sayeh's books of poetry span more than fifty years of the past century, embodying tremendous range, from the traditional Iranian forms, especially the ghazal and ruba'i, to the modern free-verse poems called *white poems*. Nobel-nominated poet Simin Behbahani writes that Sayeh's ability to master traditional styles "while maintaining the particularities of contemporary times and events is a formidable task, which necessitates great competence." The poet Mehdi Akhavan-Sales goes so far as to say, "[T]he quality of Sayeh's work is one of the reasons for the gradual triumph of free verse poetry" in Iran. Some of Sayeh's poems are inward, spare lyrics, while others are bardic incantations which seem to speak for the whole nation from a sweeping view of history. Sayeh writes love poems, philosophical meditations, elegies, and invectives of political lament. Like the great Persian Sufi poets Hafez and Rumi, a common refrain for Sayeh is wine and drunkenness, in sorrow, in cultural communion, and in ecstatic revelry—both divine and romantic—where "the whole cosmos is dancing like a drunk."

Sayeh is one of Iran's most celebrated living poets. He has been invited to read his poems in the Soviet Union, India, Germany, Austria, Canada, Tajikistan, Uzbekistan, and the United States. Born in 1928 in the northern city of Rasht, Iran, Houshang Ebtehaj published his first book of poetry, *First Songs* (1946), at the age of nineteen under the pen name "Sayeh," which means "shadow." His early work was noted for its musical qualities, directness, and unconcealed sentiment, often romantic and with a youthful passion toward social commitment and the possibilities of change. During Iran's "open period" following World War II, which supported a flowering in the arts, Sayeh became involved in Iran's literary circles and published his poems in leading magazines. The poem "Caravan" (1952) exemplifies the two-fold impulse in Sayeh's poetry during this period, a tension between the personal romantic and a widening socio-political consciousness:

> It's late, Galia!
> This is no time for kisses and love poems
> Everything has the color of fire and blood

As Sayeh developed, his poetry increasingly stretched toward the past and the future in a dual gesture, exhibiting a hybrid of contemporary poetry and traditional Iranian verse in the lineage of Persian masters Rumi and Hafez. After Hafez, Sayeh is known as the best Iranian poet of the ghazal. Poet and Persian scholar Kamyar Abedi writes that Sayeh's ghazals "are among the most successful pieces of modern Persian literature." Abedi describes the blending of personal and historic content in Sayeh's work as abiding in two primary modes, "historical-literary individual romanticism and socio-political romanticism" and as encompassing the "traditional, neo-traditional, and modern" during the great span of his literary career. Often performed with classical Persian instruments, Sayeh's bardic poetry rolls off the tongue with incantatory resonance, yet in the style of modern innovator Nima Yushij, his work emphasizes current issues of Iranian society, such as the political turmoil that resulted after the CIA-led coup d'état in 1953 and the Islamic Revolution of 1979.

The 1979 Revolution marked a turning point in Sayeh's life and art. Sayeh's long meditation, "Dance of Burning," written during the first year of the Revolution, seems a paean to cycles of change and restoration on all levels: personal, national, and cosmic. As the Revolutionary government increasingly came to reflect the will of conservative interpretations of Islam, there was intense conflict between the state and the more secular elements in Iran. Political activists and intellectuals were kidnapped from their homes in night raids called *Shabikhoon*, literally "night blood," and women were beaten or arrested for allowing their hair to show in public. Sayeh's poems gave voice to the sorrow felt by much of the nation. He was arrested in 1981 and held in prison for a year. Many of his friends and the poets in his circle were also arrested, and some were executed. Sayeh's poetry from this time forward is fraught with darker notes of disappointment, hopelessness, and sorrow—of waiting for the "lost friend" to return.

> I don't know who sold our loyalty
> What he earned or bought with the money
>
> But I see that black hand above the bar
> Pouring poison in the people's wine

Upon release from prison, Sayeh immersed himself in his most ambitious scholarly project, an exhaustive comparative study of the contrary versions of Hafez's poetry, worldwide, which culminated in the publication of *Hafez, by Sayeh* (1994). Sayeh's research led him throughout Europe, the Middle East, Tajikistan, and India to identify and gather into a definitive collection what he argued to be the true works of Hafez. From these efforts and from the philosophical and stylistic influences of Hafez, which are widely noted by scholars, Sayeh earned the nickname "the modern Hafez." Since 1987, Sayeh has lived between Cologne, Germany, and Tehran, Iran.

Mojdeh Marashi and I have translated representative poems from Sayeh's twelve books to exhibit the range of his poetic work through what we are identifying as three eras of production: 1) 1946–1970: romantic youth, the coup d'état of 1953, and the following two decades; 2) 1971–1980: Sayeh's rich middle period, showcasing significant growth and innovation in his poetry as the country moves toward and into the Revolution; 3) 1980–1996: a period defined by the aftermath of the Revolution and Sayeh's imprisonment. Mojdeh and I have learned much about our given languages and cultures, as well as the culture of the "other," because of the deep historic and linguistic struggle that these poems demand of us to bring thousands of years of event and story into English. We have often felt that there is simply no acceptable translation for a word or phrase because of the folkloric, mythic, and religious references and archetypes that whisper through the centuries from as far back as Zoroastrian Persia. As rich and as foundational to European culture as are *Oedipus Rex, King Lear,* or *Grimm's Fairy Tales,* Persian culture sings out from its own panoply of reference points, its own sense of cosmology, forged along the Silk Road at the crossroads of the world's great empires. In the way that "Out out—" evokes the tragedy of Macbeth for a European reader, a Persian reader recognizes the medieval love story of *Layla and Majnoon* or the Koranic *Joseph* at the bottom of the well. These stories are carried inside the collective spirit, and only a few Persian words are necessary to summon their emotional nuances.

As to the qualities of sound and rhythm in Sayeh's work, these poems are often performed in Persian, by Sayeh and others, to the accompaniment of Persian classical music. They are truly beautiful in their original tongue, richly textured in sound, which presents a remarkable challenge in translation. Furthermore, many of these poems follow a complex pattern of rhyme and meter in multiple traditional forms. In trying to maintain the strict formal structures of these rhymed traditions, we found the English syntax to be too stiff and unnatural, that the music and meaning of the poems were contorted. So we chose, instead, to allow image and sense to guide the process of translation, while aiming for musical *congruence*, rather than musical *equality*. Rather than a literal interpretation of rhyme scheme, especially end-rhyme, we listened for the music inherent in English—of front rhyme, internal rhyme and near rhyme, of assonance and consonance—in order to bestow congruent melodic qualities to the translations. We believe the truest translations must employ the musical capacities of English, just as the originals highlight the musical capacities of Persian. Even so, on many levels, we cannot help but mourn what is lost in the translation.

One representative challenge comes in the poem "Exiled" with the word *begardid,* whose multiple meanings Sayeh employs to great effect: *search, circle, whirl, dance, spin, swing, turn,* and *churn.* This *whirling* is the circling of the Dervish, of history, and of the planets, a turning at both micro and macro levels. Sayeh's use of the single word in multiple contexts is meant to reveal this pattern in the whole of existence. Furthermore, the poem is a ghazal, and as such the key word *begardid* repeats as the final word in each couplet, bearing one or more of its meanings with each recurrence. In a further complication, in Persian the verb (*begardid*) arrives last in the sentence. A direct translation of this leaves an awkward and flaccid syntax, the verb dragging passively at the end of each sentence, nonsensical and unmusical in English. Our translation attempts to naturalize the syntax into a musical English incantation, while honoring the ghazal structure by occasionally placing or repeating the verb *begardid* (to circle / search) last in the sentence. The latter proffers the added benefit of foreignizing and thereby enriching the English language through the inverse syntax of Persian. The result in "Exiled," if we have succeeded, is a poem which upholds some of the ghazal's formal strategies while weaving a coherent musical chant in English.

Search, search the house, look everywhere
You're an exile in this house, search like an exile

We have included here many of Sayeh's most treasured works and a representative sample from his many books, but we realize others would have selected differently and would certainly have translated differently. We have translated the short poem "Holl" (Fear) three different ways in order to hint at each poem's potential in translation. Indeed, for each poem dozens of faithful versions are possible. This is the first full-length collection of Sayeh's poems to appear in English. We hope and fully expect others will follow.

— Chad Sweeney

I

1980-1996

Gharibaaneh
EXILED

Tehran, Summer 1987

Search, search the house, look everywhere
You're an exile in this house, search like an exile

One is a meadow lark, my own heart's pair
The world is not her nest, search for the nest

One is a wine maid tipsy behind a curtain
She passed on the glass so whirl like the drunks

The joy of drunkenness hides under whose lips?
From this hand to that like a shared glass—circle

One is the starling that ate the garden of my heart
You won't find her in a trap—search for the seeds

A wind from her mouth has caught me in fragrance
She is here, she is here, search the whole house

A song no one heard, it fled from itself
Don't call out its name, go softly, go softly

Tears planted in that dirt grow the root of the vine
In the turbulence of wine, churn in the cellar

What a sweet smell, where is her bed?
Circle that flower as a butterfly—search

Laugh at the intellect that love didn't choose it
Swing in these chains like a lunatic—search

Her footprint's not here in these walls built of sorrow
If you hunger for treasure, search in the ruins

If a door opens inward, you are the key
Turn like the gears in a lock made of time

Who veiled her face from Sayeh under a spell of sleep?
In dreams you can't find her, search in the legends

Her body brushed my body, she took me, she took me
If she never brings me back, go with gratitude, whirling

Sayeh: In Persian, Sayeh means "shadow." In the Persian tradition of self-reference, the poet's name often appears in the final lines of the poems. In this poem "Sayeh" doubles for "shadow," invoking the poet's name and the word "shadow" at the same time. This double invocation occurs in many of the poems collected here, where either the word "shadow" or Sayeh's name appear.

Zendegie
LIFE

Tehran, Winter 1992

Do you think life is a sail
planted in mud?
Has the color of fate drained
from this shipwreck,
life halted on a dead road?

A flood of accident
opened its mouth like a dragon,
cleaving the sky loose at the horizon.
Baskets and baskets of stars fell
and the sun drowned in purple valleys.

Which wind carries you
in this terrible weather?
Which cloud anchors your chest
that after a thousand years of torrential rain
your heart does not pull free?

Through millennia you rose
up this throat cave, this blood tunnel,
an unbroken trail of footprints
through this grotto of devils where your steps
echoed discovery on all sides.

Between mountain and valley a borderless pasture
where fame and disgrace signed your faithful letter in blood.
And your inspired chisel resonated in the ear
of Bistoon Castle.
Many lashes tested your body's will to love,
hanging ropes stretched your neck proud.
How glorious was the spine of love
that stood tall against every abuse?

Look
to that high place:
                    dawn's blooming plain, an eruption of light
                              draws hope toward it,
           fire the human soul stretches toward.

          For the scent of one breath in that transparency of breathing
          I would fall
          a thousand times from the hillroad
          only to turn again toward that height.

          Do you think
          the world's a broken mirror
          where even the cypress appears crooked?
          The way this mountain watches the valley
          like a hunter in tumultuous dusk—
          to you the road's an avalanche.

Time stretches without coastlines—
the steps of our lives can't measure it.
This shelter from pain is only a moment.

As the river
strikes the rock slope of the canyon,
        stay steady,
the dead man has no hope for a miracle—
        stay alive.

Shabikhoon

NIGHT RAID

Tehran, Summer 1980

Hurry wine maid, serve the glass—sorrow unveils its face!
What catastrophe has ambushed us again?

My heart's image floats in the goblet, wine maid,
We must see what color this indigo wheel is bringing

We placed one hundred hopes in our friend, wine maid,
But did you catch him wet his fingers in our heartblood?

The altar fire was snuffed out by that devil's breath
Even as he blew smoke into his own eyes, wine maid

The universe is thirsty for our planet's blood, wine maid,
And this new moon's an old scythe cutting what we planted

I owe nothing, wine maid, if he grants one more dawn or dusk
No difference subtracted from him or added to me

I've washed my soul's garment in the bloody well of the liver
So much, wine maid, its cross-weaves have unraveled

In love's shrine, wine maid,
The heart was right to bow only for you

Lips and grail were shaped for churning wine
Without wine there's no use for mouth or glass

Close the door, wine maid—like a shadow in solitude
I don't want to talk to anyone

Shadow: also "Sayeh" the poet's name

Night Raid: In Persian "Shabikhoon" literally translates to "nightblood" which recalls raids and kidnappings of political enemies under the cover of night.

Bar Aastaan-e Vaafa

AT THE SHRINE OF LOYALTY

Tehran, Winter 1984

Who are you that without you my heart is a windy swing
and thoughts scatter leaves over sleepless eyes?

Who'll carry the news to citizens in safety
They are boats once more rocked in turbulent water?

I've lost faith in the measure of the world
The fortunes of the kind are only reflections on a wave

Keep this tenderness hidden in your chest
One-thousand arrows wait to ambush your loved ones

Hold the heart steady for this mirror, if you can,
Even as the image trembles like mercury

I've bowed our hands to the shrine of loyalty
If there's any hope left, it'll be here

All other grails have left me in withdrawal
I'm loyal to this woman whose wine is ambrosia

Don't harbor hope for the torchbearer of the sky
This prison niche is no place for the moon

Time levels hard payment for injustice
The reward for an unlucky Rosttam is his dead son, Sohraab

Eagles stretch their wings in the sky
Pity this show of flight is only a pattern in a frame

In your longing, in the end, all will be lost
Scattered like the soul of a shadow

Rosttam and Sohraab: In the *Shahnameh*, (Book of Kings) the epic hero Rosttam meets his son, Sohraab, in battle, and after failing to recognize him, he kills him. Scholars have considered this legend in relation to Oedipus, who mistakenly kills his own father.

Ah-e Ayeneh

MOAN OF THE MIRROR

Tehran, Autumn 1982

Searching among the bodies
the family knew it was her
by her long hair.

O earth—
is this the same innocent body?
Is a woman only this pile of dirt?

She used to comb
the treasure of that hair
and braid beyond the mirror frame
the wind of her thoughts.

She greeted the morning, *Salaam!*
And her smile would pick a flower
from the reflection.
Lifting her hand to her temple
she would sweep the night aside
to reveal
the sun in the mirror.

Her mind would wake on the rising day,
a rain of stars shaking loose
from the sky of her eyes,
then that kind smile
would open a door through her reflection
onto the sun-garden of her soul.

Thieves have blinded the mirror
by stealing those eyes
from the sill of morning.

You—burnt youth—

                spring ash!
Your image has fled from the mirror.
Framing the memory of your long hair
the mirror moans in the hanging dust of morning.

Birds in the garden sing for no reason.
This is no occasion for bloom.

After the Revolution of 1979, there were so many killings that families searched for the
missing in mass graves at the edges of cities.

Arghavaan
ARGHAVAAN

Arghavaan is a tree whose large crimson flowers appear in early
spring before any leaves have sprouted. The flowers fall around
the foot of the tree and stain the ground red. While in prison,
Sayeh had a vision of the arghavaan tree at his family house in
Tehran.

Tehran, Spring 1984

Arghavaan, my one-blood, my cut branch!
What color is your sky today?
Sunny
or locked in cloud?

In this corner outside of the world
no sun yellows my forehead,
no news arrives from the spring.
All I know is wall,
the dark so close
when I empty my lungs
the air returns against me,
the flight of the eye
stumbles a single step.

A thin flame from a sick lamp
is the only storyteller tonight.
My breath catches,
the air, too, is prisoner.

Whatever remains of me
has lost the color of its face.
The sun has not dropped one
glance from the rim of its eye
into the amnesia of this vault.

From quiet oblivion
in whose cold air every candle dies,
a vision of color kindles the mind,
                out there, my arghavaan:
my arghavaan is alone,
my arghavaan cries
with this flayed heart
bleeding from the eyes.

Arghavaan,
what is the secret that spring always
arrives carrying our grief?
That every year the sand stains
with the blood of swallows
and over the branded heart heaps
loss onto loss?

Arghavaan, earth's claw,
grab hold the morning's robes and ask
the galloping messengers of the sun

when they will cross this black valley.

Arghavaan, hung in clusters of blood-fruit,
at dawn when doves
riot the windowsill of sunrise,
lift my petaled soul
in your fingers,
hoist it to the flight's watchtowers.
Hurry, the flock is
grieving for captive birds.

Arghavaan—spring's banner of flowers,
raise your colors!
Become my bleeding poem.

Keep the memory of my loved ones
red on your tongue.

Shout the poem I cannot write!
Arghavaan, my one-blood,

              my cut branch.

Shomareh
NUMBER

Tehran, 1983

Fallen from above as the dust of the door
Like a shadow at noon I've dwindled to nothing
Yesterday, a husband, a father, a brother
Now I'm reduced to this numeral 10

Gham-e Shir

SORROW OF THE LION

Tehran, Spring 1983

In the corner of the cage the lion is broken
The tyrant's rope upon his neck
And in his wet eyes the shadow of the forest
Oh god, what sorrow!

Zendaan
JAIL

Tehran, Summer 1983

In old age pain and sadness is my jail
Just being old earns two hundred times the suffering
I'm devoted to the sage who said,
The whole world is a prison for the wise

Honar-e Gaam-e Zamaan

THE ART OF STEPPING THROUGH TIME

Tehran, Fall 1983

The world does not begin or end today
Sad and happy hide behind one curtain

If you're on the path don't despair of the distance
Arrival is the art of stepping through time

A seasoned traveler on the road to love's door
Your blood leaves its mark on every step

Still water soon sinks into the earth
But the river rolling grows into a sea

Let's hope one reaches the target
So many arrows have flown from this old bow

Time taught me to fall out of love with your face
That's why my tears are tinted with blood

Shame this long game of decades
Plays the human heart a toy

A caravan of tulips crossing this meadow
Was crushed under hoof by the riders of autumn

The day that sets spring's breath in motion
Will birth flowers and grasses from shore to shore

Mountain, you heard my cry today
The ache in this chest was born with the world

All praised brotherhood but did not live it
God, how many miles from tongue to hand?

Blood trickles my eyes in this corner of enduring
The patience I practice is squeezing my life

Come on, Sayeh, don't swerve from the path
A jewel is buried beneath every step

Ghorrob-e Chaman

SUNSET ON THE GREEN

Tehran, Fall 1989

Tell me under dusk the grieving green of meadows.
This sadness of tousled grasses, tell.

Look to ashen dreams of the arghavaan,
Wordlessly confess the thoughts of the burned.

What became of her face leaned on the young tree sprout?
Tell the dirt's embrace. Tell the solitude of the rose.

The joy of first green left the old tree's memory.
O spring wind, please tell of those days.

Water won't return to a dry creek bed.
Let wet eyes tell of the thirst of the jasmine.

Tell the crowds struck silent with grief
Of the wine maids' festivals of morning wine.

Tell of the messenger, a hundred flowers on his chest
And this wave of blood that slaps him on the mouth.

The broken pine sketched my heart on the water.
Tell this story to the heartbreaking mirror.

That green and red Sayeh turned amethyst and bruise.
My night pine, tell of sunset on the green.

Tasvir

IMAGE

Tehran, Fall 1989

The house is empty
like the mirror without an image
in a night of waiting.

A picture hangs on the wall,
a green memory
traced in the mind of an autumn night.

A girl,
head held high, a pouring of long hair.
A boy,
his face in quiet anguish for a father
and a graceful woman, but far away . . . .

In a night of waiting, a man,
the mirror without an image,
the empty house.

A shadow throbs in the mirror's pit—
a hundred images
can't replace what's missing,
the whisper of footsteps on the rug.

The one crying with you is the mirror.
You are this lonely face.

Kahrobaa
TOPAZ

Tehran, Summer 1983

I don't mean to go, she is pulling me
As topaz draws a bewildered straw

When I twist my collar free from her claw
She seizes the tails of my robes

When I flail to get clear, she grabs my jaw
As I free my head, she catches my leg

Please, I beg, release me from this love
If I let go, she says, loyalty will hold you

Your ear drowses under the tongue, I say,
To lure my unspoken words from hiding

But first, she answers, my secret power of smell
Will decipher the scent of your thoughts in the air

She's become the joy of bread under my tooth
My wheat is pulling me toward her mill

I'm her shadow now, how can I escape?
I'll follow wherever she leads

Siyah o Sephid

BLACK AND WHITE

Cologne, Germany, Summer 1991

Such a night has arrived that a thousand lifetimes
Must pass before the sun will breathe again

Doubt guards the doorframe of dawn
Where a sunless sky paints me black

The morning star has shifted a thousand years away
Do you see what is happening to the world?

A shout for what lives have drown in this ocean
Squandered in diving for pearls

No seashell hides the jewel we're looking for
Raise a glass for your tears, drunk on the liquor of hope

I don't know who sold our loyalty
What he earned or bought with the money

But I see that black hand above the bar
Pouring poison in the people's wine

Is it right for a friend's rib to leak blood
For not discerning the gilt of a blade?

What patterns have you ruined in painting our time
White for black and black for white?

Come on, who'll follow love singing from the road?
Our lives are hostages listening for the call

Let's go, the world depends on this
It's the magic that tends the essential fire

Sayeh's soul holds the mirror of the sun
Look into his night where no dawn blows

Chadin Hezar Omid-e Bani Aadam

THE FEW THOUSAND HOPES
OF THE CHILDREN OF ADAM

Tehran, Winter 1992

What a nice surprise, I said with a buoyant heart
But the drunk at the door I recognized as sorrow

The eye of the garden couldn't see my dark tear
Because the dew on the flower was empty of stars

Fluttering her feathers, the butterfly slept in her own trap
Night wound to its end in the silk cocoon

What stormclouds have locked us in again?
Not only me, the whole world is surrounded

You've stolen my religion, what are you doing?
You've branded my spirit, though it meant so little to you

Your pick is strumming the wrong direction
Harpist of time—which is up, which is down?

Pause to notice what you're losing to the wind
The few thousand hopes of the children of Adam

You say Sayeh's poetry wears the color of mourning
Yes, one hundred deaths are woven in this robe

Baal-e Kabutar
DOVE'S WINGS

Tehran, Fall 1986

Night was pounding its head with black hands.
Someone far away, a dove fluttering,
> the music of Iran, Baal-e Kabutar!

The bird mourned on a branch,
my heart beating its wings for you.

Baal-e Kabutar, literally "dove's wings," is a motif in Persian classical music.

Taasian

TAASIAN

Tehran, Fall 1996

The house was ailing for the vanishing sun,
as now my heart is sick.

Father told us to light the lamp,
and night filled with night.

I was certain the sun was lost,
but Mother sighed,
Morning will bring it back.

A cloud drifted my young eyes
into sleep.

Who knew this much suffering
crept in ambush toward a child's heart?

Yes, in those days when someone left us
I had faith in his return.

I hadn't swallowed the meaning
of never.

O doomed word,
my heart has not grown accustomed to you.

Why haven't they come back?

After all these years I
still fix my eyes on the road

waiting.

II

1971-1980

Falgh

RED DAWN

Tehran, 1971

O dawn!
The messenger's happy news!
To honor your visit tonight
a rooster
is beheaded at the front door.

Saboohi

MORNING WINE

for Khosrow Golesorkhi, executed under the Shah

Tehran, February 18, 1974

He lifted the sky
in an ebony bowl.
The red dawn
drank it down in one swallow.
In that moment the sun blazed
through his entire being.

Hameesh-e Dar Miyan
ALWAYS IN BETWEEN

Tehran, Spring 1976

The ones-yet-to-come and the already-gone are running towards you
From two continents of time—you who are always in between

In your pasture the deer of the sky are grazing
The white eagle of the universe circles your head

I look around in this field
The mind's mirror reflects nothing but you

You are nature's flower, please lower your veil
Your dawn vapor draws me to the garden

You've kept hidden, an oasis in a fruit pit
If I split the seed your orchard sprouts out

You've become drunk with desire for me
Then pulled your teasing curtain aside

You sprouted from within yourself
And because you did the world began

A wave of blood breaks from the mind
What can I do, you aim the bow from inside me?

In your presence there's no discord between life and death
Your breath is the incense of living the moment

In your presence my clothes scream to be torn away
I try to know you, but ceaseless crying prevents me

Khaab
SLEEP

Tehran, July 2, 1971

I'm crying while I write this!

From sleep
I woke up crying
my hand still

resting on your long
                              neck
the smell of your black hair
                          tangling

with my lips
Is it possible . . .
                    I woke with a cry

Gheseh
STORY

Tehran, September 13, 1971

Reed flute, my heart is wailing low
O God, again, which lover's blood
trickles into the well?

Diyr
LATE

Tehran, Winter 1971

Youth is a shimmering image
The heart eventually lets it go
Startled from sweet morning sleep
Come, my heart, it's late

Hesaar
WALLS

"Hesaar" refers specifically to prison walls or castle walls.

Tehran, Spring 1978

O lovers, lovers, fill your goblets with blood
From your cardial blood, tint your cheeks like tulips

Here comes someone riding the fire—abandon these walls
For a new sun to rise, cast this night from you

Why such a sigh in the house of allies?
Lift the moon of Joseph's face up from sorrow's well

Steady the mirror of our eyes before his luminous face
Draw this tragic beauty into your command

The man in his tempest rends the shackles and the cell
From a lock of Layla's hair, tie a ring for Majnoon's neck

I saw in a dream at midnight the sun and moon touch
Waking at dawn, how do you interpret this?

Radiance for friends and smoke for enemies
I feed my heart to the fire—so pile on more wood

How long will blood leak from this dishonored throne?
Deconstruct this throne, hoist the crown upside down

Our hearts pour as we pour from cask to goblet
All who witness the festival of hatred—fill your goblets with blood

Layla and Majnoon: A famous medieval love story. Majnoon was madly in love with Layla.

Kayvaan Setarch Bood

KAYVAAN WAS A STAR

Kayvaan, a beloved figure and friend of Sayeh, was killed by the Shah's
government after the coup d' état of 1953. The name "Kayvaan" also
means "Venus" the morning star.

Tehran, June 17, 1979

We were from the fire's race,
born the same hour as the copper sun
yet darkened in ash.

Injustice smoldered in its forge,
my friend vanished like a spark,
I stayed behind with the patience of coal.

Kayvaan became a star
so above the grave night
hope
would shine for us.

Kayvaan became a star
so the beaten-down
could trace the path to dawn.

Kayvaan became a star
                    to teach us
about fire,
the moment it flares

inside the self
and illuminates the evening.

Shaabe yalda, the longest night,
my palms tired of hoping
placed in his bright hands.

Shaabe yalda, solstice night,
my faith in the sun stays lit
by the color of his star.

Kayvaan, the star of morning,
he lived the way of light
and died by light.

He sits in the pupil of our eyes,
an heirloom of fire
handed to the sun for holding.

Parandeh Midaanad
THE BIRD KNOWS

Tehran, 1971

Thoughts of flying in cloud light
like opening an eye into sleep
the bird in her cage
       is dreaming.

From her cage the bird watches
the painted image of the garden
shimmer.
The bird knows this wind
has no breath—the paradise
an illusion!
From her cage the bird
       is dreaming.

Soghoot
THE FALL

Tehran, 1971

He used to stretch his neck up
higher than the world!

The stars that glitter the wheel
would kiss his fingertips.
The sun was a coin
in his fist.

At times
a universe separates
a crown from its shoulders.

At times pride and humiliation
differ the width of a hair.

When he bowed in resignation
the sky and its stars
removed beyond all reach.

Entezaar
WAIT

Tehran, Spring 1978

Come, my love, the heart can't be corked
My soul has risen to the lips to wait for you

In the heat of withdrawal, there's nothing I can do
But tip back your grail again, again

Get ready, wine maid, for this drunk who worships wine
As the barrel waits for wine to ripen, I wait in withdrawal for you

On all sides the chaos of history
The only calm is when we're together

There's no relief for this fevered throat
Not even when tasting your well's sweet water

The heart's shanty was pillaged by love
Eyes, bleed your tears, this civil war is your doing

The hope of flowering never left my old heart
Its dried branch survives by the vapor of your spring

Wait, Sayeh, keep on waiting—
What the heart aches for will come

Geryeh-e Seeb

APPLE'S CRY

Tehran, Spring 1972

Night was falling.
I came inside and closed the windows.

Wind wrestled with branches.
Only me in an empty house.

The world's lament poured into my heart.

Suddenly I felt
someone
                    beyond the window
in the garden
                              crying,

morning dew
                    dropped
from the apple blossom.

Baazgasht
RETURN

Tehran, October 25, 1973

A nest is empty without its bird,
but emptier still is the nest of a bird
whose mate has been kept away.

Oh broken white wings of doves
welcome home to your nests!
But my heart is still captive
with those who flew beside you,
those birds
who never returned . . . .

Aan Eshgh

THAT LOVE

Tehran, Fall 1975

That love by which eyes learn to cry
and the soul sink and smolder.

Look at me!
Memory

and ache,
what more have I won from love?

Beytol Ghazal
HOUSE OF GHAZAL

Tehran, Summer 1975

What love is this love? We don't know what it is.
It's sane and insane, yet neither sanity nor insanity.

How can a madman or sage understand
The drunkenness of this grail increases every day?

When the sea is wild, the moon's reflection is obscured
By this wave of mercury rising up, sinking down

Imagination and feeling hold the intellect captive
Like a deer in whose presence the lion is helpless

Where is the blade that opened the vessel of the soul
And can no longer hide the twilight of the wound?

When you arced your eyebrow I almost lost my mind
Imagine what your whole eye could do, your house of ghazal

What would I make with a lock of that hair?
The strands of such thread are beyond comprehension

Sayeh, we're not talking about delicacy of the body
But she who is all soul inside her clothing

So get up in a frenzy, clasp onto her hair
This is what you've been waiting for

Wearing earth-rags, you're trying to charm the sun
Hold up your face until she is your mirror

Samaa-e Sokhtan

DANCE OF BURNING

Tehran, Winter 1980

Love is joy, love is freedom
Love is humanity's seed

Love tends a fire in the chest
Your breath stokes it with your intentions

Love is the heat that multiplies itself
The birth of a birthing cosmos

Inside the seed the whole garden pulses
In the night of the cocoon is the butterfly's dance

A ripple in the hidden curtain of the soul
Encodes life with its design

What is life but this practice of loving?
To give ourselves wholly to it?

One who loves is truly alive
The soul and heart are made worthy by love

Think of yourself as a spark
That worships light and can become light

You burn to illuminate what's around you—
Revel all night to share a bed with dawn

Love is the glow of this magic lamp
That abides in fire and creates fire

Without the liquid transparency of this fire
You're a fistful of dirt, antipathy and corruption

Crude pitch, dawn captured in mud
Beauty with rock eyes and rock heart

Listen, lovely woman, whether devil or angel
Without light you can only be shadow

The sun has planted its burn in you
Yet your wood hasn't spun any flame?

You rose like a tree, don't fade like coal—
Blaze like a ripening fruit

When fruit rounds into its aurora
It offers this nectar of ripeness

The fruit of this tree is not apple or quince
In the end its fruit will be fire

Wet or dry, everything in the world
Shares the essence of burning

This burning is the will to become light
Weightless and free from its form

. . .

Even the mountain was a conflagration
Gushing and raining when the world began

Fire and music like the sky—
Whose cold breath cooled it to stone?

Light is prisoner in this body
Dense and cold are not the nature of granite

Rock is disappointed with its fate
The will to motion remains in its core

Until a forge heats the granite to melting
And returns its soul of going . . .

. . .

When you strike two rocks
They spark fire between them

In the night of a tryst the eye
Sparks smiles on the lovers' mouths

Laughter is the glow on a young face
Rippling as moon over water

What is light but the laughter of Being?
Laughter drunk on its own joy?

So excited by this glee
The whole cosmos whirls like a drunk

Light has twirled in seven curtains
Before coming to circle in this mirror

Color is the raiment, the red and the white,
But the nude body of light is invisible

A few starlings sit on that low branch—
How many starlings are in the whole tree?

That little blackness is all they are
But they overwhelm the sky when they fly . . .

. . .

You gathered-and-stored atoms to make your body
And separated yourself from me

A body yearns to be with another body
One looking-for-a-mate is a lonely number

You were a river in motion tossing all about you—
Why did you settle into a motionless sea?

Each of your atoms was an expanding sun
But you stored them away in a room of smoke

Are you a brick-maker for bodies? Why wait any longer?
Come out from that shed of mixing the clay

East and West stretch the boundaries of self
Sky and Earth trace the circle of your arms . . .

. . .

The red flower like boiled blood
Has drunk the splendor of the sun

Who distills rose water from that flower
Is milking the sun's essence

Now the soul of the sun is corked in a bottle
A bottle which ponders the thinness of its glass

The rose water's fragrance is the genie of its soul
How it hurries to escape from the bottle!

. . .

Tulips are messengers from the sun's garden
They stitch a little light into dirt

Because they've carried this ancient letter
They'll circle their way back to the sun

. . .

The measure of light that each leaf absorbs
Is returned when the leaf falls away

The branch busies with the work of making cloth
The dance of burning in its mind

This antler of wood is only a borrower
It must pay back its debt in radiance

. . .

Inside the seed, a meeting of friends
Like a night for tributes adorned in candles

Color, incense, design—all gather here
Until dawn releases them into the flower

The petal's make-up artist applies shade and beauty
By limning the patterns of the sun

The flower is the answer to the sun's bright word
One friend smiles into another friend's face

. . .

Supple and delicate a sapling
Threads its head through the ice of the earth

Its green eye inclined toward the sun
Long ago dreamed of fire

In its center a sigh has waited
The sun's mane tossed in its breathing

The sun is drawn to this seed as well
A shard of her own heart of light

Through its season in the soil
The seed carries memories of the sun

And reading to the end
Finds the destiny of the tree it will become

Though it sways and flirts in the meadow
The destiny of the tree is to burn

. . .

The ancient tree is me—time has wheeled
Over many autumns and springs

My hands and pockets are empty and my feet are tied
But I'm lifting my crown toward open sky

The starless nights are tomb nights
Yet in my heart a distant star

On occasion a meteor took aim
Or hail froze and flailed me

A crow wove its nest over my name
And blackened the sky with its wings

A nightingale crooned with my heart
Then left behind an empty nest

Some deer got lost in the meadow's night
A cry for those that never returned

It's true I grew no fruit or flowers
But my shadow was refuge for a few

The ax of the lumberjack struck
And the wood inhaled its final smoke

I'm an ancient trunk that contemplates fire
Wishing it were my own fire

III

1946-1970

Mardjaan

CORAL

Tehran, Winter 1954

A rock under waves
in the blue night of the sea
alone in a grave's hollow
in the quiet cold.
Abandoned
to prison silence
the sun never reaches it,
moon never sets it glowing.
What it says to the dark
no one hears,
many evenings it weeps
into the red abyss.
Mineral under tides, furrowed stone,
alive, throbbing hope in the deep—
in the chest of a loved one, it would be a heart,
in the shadow of the sun, it would be a flower.

Gholhaa-ye Yaas

JASMINE FLOWERS

Rasht, August 19, 1946

Whose were those strands of jasmine last night
Asleep on your lovely chest?
Somehow you guessed my secret wish
To hang down from your neck

With that insinuating smile
The honeyed gaze that stirs me
You loosened the clasp from your neck
And offered the fragrant jasmine

I kissed them many times in your absence
Lost my heart and became drunk
In awe I smelled the flowers
And plummeted into their smell

Your jasmine slept beside me
In bed till sunrise
Releasing its incense all night
The bed was full of your smoke

I marveled at that fragrance
Vining from such small petals!
I pondered the enigma
Of their rapturous bloom

Ah ha!—you witching fruit blossom!
I found the source of your spell
Amid the bundle of jasmine petals
A single strand of your hair

Marg-e Rooz
DEATH OF THE DAY

Tehran, Summer 1948

The sun departed, dragging behind
the half-dead day with its skirts of dying light.
Day fell from the blade,
crawled after its lover like a fluttering heart.

Why whimper? the sun laughed,
Be glad this bruising hour is over.
Smile and exalt—why should you complain,
We're both leaving this place?

The tired day moaned back, You're the king of light!
Happiness is yours, not mine.
We're stepping off this bad road together
But you to the wedding bed and I to the grave.

Naaghoos
BELL

Rasht, Spring 1952

A bell sounded in my chest.
I startled from sleep
and jumped up:
        "What was that!? What was it?
A bell for love or death?"
No lips opened to answer me.

A gust of wind killed the lantern.
Night spread like a terrible dream.
The bell tolled in my chest.
I asked myself,
"What's that song?
For whom is the bell ringing?"

Ehsaas
FEELING

Tehran, Winter 1953

My bed
is the empty shell of loneliness.
You are the pearl
strung from other men's necks.

Karevaan

CARAVAN

Tehran, Winter 1953

It's late, Galia!
Don't sing a love story in my ear!
And don't ask for passionate ghazals!
It's late, Galia, the caravan has started to move

Our love for each other? . . . Yes,
That's a story, too,
But as long as our people grope for the night's bread
There's no time for stories or romance

Blooming on the twilight of your birthday
Your glow lights twenty candles
Yet the same night a thousand girls your age
Sleep hungry and naked on the ground

While the dance and tease of your fingers
Float over sitar strings
A thousand weaver girls
With bloody, infected fingers
Die slowly, the soul unraveling from the body
In the tight cage of the workshop
For less pay than you would toss to a beggar's lap

And this seven-color carpet crushed beneath your dance
Has earned its prism from the blood of human beings
In the warp and weft of each line and figure: a thousand sufferings
In the design of each flower and leaf: a thousand shames

Here a thousand innocent hopes have slept buried in earth
And the wind has swept away a thousand young fires
Here the hands of a thousand blameless children
The ruined eyes of a thousand sick girls . . .

It's late, Galia!
This is no time for kisses and love poems
Everything has the color of fire and blood
It's the revolution of voices and hands
It's the revolution of life

Don't smile in my face!
From now on your gaze
Is forbidden—so is wine and love!
And the drumming of a happy heart!

My friends are bound in wet dark
Dungeons at the Shah's palace
In fevered exile at Khark Island
At each edge and corner of this black hell

It's early, Galia!

Don't sing a love story in my ear!

And don't ask for songs of passion

It's early, Galia! The caravan has not arrived . . .

The same day the pearled arms of dawn

Swing a scimitar to tear the night's curtain,

The day the sun

Flickers through each crack in the wall

And the cheeks of war-tired friends

Find again the colors of laughter

I'll be back on that day

To songs and ghazals and kisses

To the fertile, heart-thawing spring

And to you

              my love

Faryaad
SCREAM

A few months after the coup d'état,
Tehran, October 1953

A wail from everyone murdered in the city
Like a fog lifting from the tulip field
Tomorrow, when they blow the horns for Judgment Day
The thousand-year scream will rise

Ghorbat
EXILE

Tehran, Fall 1953

I wail like the flute
in the burn of loss—Ah, little breeze
of the familiar! So dust-veiled in exile
I don't recognize where I'm from

Setarvan
STERILE

Tehran, Fall 1953

In our orchard of no trees
who planted this ax in place of a flower?
Such dragon-wood from hell
that sprawled everywhere and took root?
Hear me, this omen of sterility
will never pollinate the spring.
No flower can rise from it,
no nightingale can sing.

Shayad . . .

MAYBE . . .

Tehran, April 24, 1952

Open the door
hurry! Get the candles
light some incense
pull the curtains from the moon's face . . .

Maybe
this dust wandering the road
is the lost friend

Hanooz
YET

Although you have turned up the dust in me
And doused me in a rain of misfortune
You do not wash out from my eyes with the tears
You cling like a sigh to the ghost of my heart

Chang-e Hozin

SAD HARP

Tehran, Fall 1953

I dreamed she was seated in sadness
A harp in her arms—unstrung!
Chang-e hozin, I know this sad harp
O my love, my broken love

Sobh-e Arezoo

MORNING OF WISH

Tehran, Winter 1954

O I'll wake up that morning
And escape the bed to be in your arms
And throw open the door to you, and kiss
Your face, in ecstasy, and throw flowers at your feet

Omid
HOPE

Tehran, Autumn 1953

What luster in the pupils of night
Lit a new glow in my light
O owl, don't croon your ominous lullaby
Behind curtains the sun is still white

Tanhaee

LONELINESS ·

Tehran, Autumn 1953

Morning rose and the dawn bird called
The black sky spread her golden skirts
One of these evenings, you said you would come
The nights keep passing and my arms are empty

Sang
STONE

Tehran, Fall 1953

Dawn stirred the flower's colors
But when I looked again she was pale
Just playing shy, I thought
I reached out to touch a stone

Shekasteh

BROKEN

Rasht, Spring 1954

Your eyes are ill and tired, my dove.
Who broke your wing?
What happened to your high-flying arc?
O sublime white, who shackled your feet?

Bafah
LESSON IN LOYALTY

Tehran, October 19, 1954

Fire, you are dim yet apt to flare
Treasure, you are squandered yet safe
We learn from your loyalty and love
Your life and your death are teachers

Holl

Three versions of the poem "Holl."

Tehran, Fall 1956

FRIGHT

Again the storm of night is.
Against the window danger bangs its fist.
The flame shivers in singularity.
Will the wind kill this lantern?

FEAR

Another storm tonight.
Fright rattles its fist on the pane.
The flame trembles of loneliness.
The wind.

DANGER

A night storm.
Danger raps its knuckle on the glass.
The wick quivers in solitude.
How can the lantern stay lit?

Dar Koocheh Saar-e Shab

NIGHT'S ALLEY

Tehran, Winter 1959

No one knocks at this empty house
No wing moves in a colorless meadow

Tangled in shadow no one raises a lantern
In night's alley no door opens to dawn

I wait for the dust that stirs without riders
But the sun can't climb from a night like this

This crossroad offers no direction but grief
No one calls *come eat!* to a passing friend

My heart can't burn any more than it's broken
Not even your knife cuts deeper

What do you expect to see with your eyes closed?
You may as well go, no one talks to deaf ears

I can offer no shade or fruit, they have the right to chop me down
But who would cut into a green living tree?

Baang-e Darya
SONG OF THE SEA

Anzali, Summer 1963

The chest should be open like the sea
To make the music the sea makes
Breath threshed like a wave
Drops a hundred times and wells up
A patient storm-weathered vessel
Not weary from rising and falling
The ballad of an oceanic heart
Not every chest can sing this way

Geryeh
CRY

Tehran, Spring 1965

Shadows sob under trees in the green sunset.
Branches read the story of clouds,
and like me, the sky is moody with dust.

Wind brings the smell of soil wet with storm.
Leaves agitate in the passing night.

The garden is anxious for rain—
my heart aches for a long green cry . . . .

Bord
TOOK

If I drank my heart's blood in vain, so I drank it
And counted so many moons and suns that I died
If it was all defeat, yes, my whole life
At least I touched your hair, yes I did

Zendeginameh

BIOGRAPHY

Tehran, Winter 1968

Memories in heaps
Crowd my head with life stories
Only in echoes of longing
The tired ghosts return

Sorkh o Sepheed
RED AND WHITE

Tehran, 1970

Until she stops weaving her long hair

at dawn

with the red corn-poppy

      she won't smile again into the mirror

Tarh
DESIGN

Tehran, 1970

They cut the morning bird's throat
   and yet

in the rolling river of sunset
    his crimson voice
  still flows . . .

The Author

H. E. Sayeh, (Houshang Ebtehaj) is one of the most important Iranian poets of the twentieth century. His many books exhibit a hybrid of contemporary and traditional Iranian verse in the lineage of Persian masters, Rumi and Hafez, though in the style of modern innovator, Nima Yushij, his work emphasizes current issues of Iranian society, especially the national crises which followed the CIA led coup d'état of 1953 and the Islamic Revolution of 1979. Sayeh's books of poetry include *First Songs* (1946), *Mirage* (1951), *Rehearsals in Caligraphy* (1953), *Earth* (1955), *Pages from the Longest Night* (1965), *Rehearsals in Caligraphy II* (1973), *Until the Dawn of the Longest Night* (1981), *Memorial to the Blood of the Cypress* (1981), *Rehearsals in Caligraphy III* (1985), *Rehearsals in Caligraphy IV* (1992), *Mirror in Mirror, Selected Poems* (Edited by M.R. Shafii-Kadkani, 1995), and *Rehearsals in Caligraphy V* (1999). Sayeh lives alternately in Cologne, Germany and in Tehran, Iran.

The Translators

Mojdeh Marashi is a writer, artist, and designer whose work is deeply influenced by the ancient and modern history of Iran. Born in Iran, she moved to U.S. in 1977 and has been based in the San Francisco Bay Area since. Filled with a deep longing for the culture she was raised in, she co-founded YALDA cultural organization in 1986, teaching Persian language classes and co-hosting the weekly radio program "Rang aa Rang (Colorful)" on KUSF, the University of San Francisco's radio station. She has an MA in Interdisciplinary Arts and an MA in Creative Writing from San Francisco State University. Her fiction was chosen for the anthology *Let Me Tell You Where I've Been: Women of the Iranian Diaspora* (University of Arkansas, 2006), and her translations (with Chad Sweeney) have appeared in *Crazyhorse, Indiana Review, Poetry International, American Letters & Commentary, Atlanta Review, Seattle Review, Subtropics* and *Washington Square*. She has traveled twice to Iran to work directly with H.E. Sayeh for this project.

Chad Sweeney is the author of four books of poetry, including *Parable of Hide and Seek* (Alice James, 2010), *Arranging the Blaze* (Anhinga, 2009), and *Wolf Milk* (Forklift Books, 2012). Sweeney's poems have appeared widely, including in *Best American Poetry, The Pushcart Prize Anthology* and Garrison Keillor's *Writer's Almanac*. He is an Assistant Professor of English at California State University, San Bernardino. He lives in Redlands with his wife, poet Jennifer K. Sweeney and their son Liam.